David Cassidy: Crazy Over You in Saratoga

Ain't no rock'n'roll story – it's a special tribute to a music legend's love of horses and the fans he loved

By Marlene Habib

Copyright © May 18, 2018 Marlene Habib

All rights reserved.

ISBN:1717235522
ISBN-13:9781717235527

DEDICATION
Get it up for love

For David Cassidy (April 12, 1950 – Never Gone), who not only sang the songs that made the whole world sing, but who also wrote many of them – and is now plucking a heavenly guitar with pal John Lennon and beloved David Bowie. For the fans and everyone in the entertainment and horse-racing communities who propped DC up when others wouldn't; for all the brave souls living with Alzheimer's-dementia as well as their loved ones, and the researchers trying to help all of us remember why I wrote this tribute book in the first place; and for my daughter Enessa, who taught me 24 hours of natural labour is nothing compared to the pain of losing someone you love.

'I've done an enormous amount of bringing light into people's lives, and I'm very proud of that, and touching and inspiring people.' -David Cassidy

---

SPECIAL THANKS
You met me more than halfway

To Cate Johnson and Brien Bouyea at the National Museum of Racing and Hall of Fame (NMRHOF) for helping David Cassidy's fans realize their goal to honour his legacy, and for arranging my special bench sneak preview (in spite of Mother Nature) so I could get this tribute book together; to the Brentwood Hotel staff, including Molly and Michaella, for making this Toronto gal feel at home and letting me spin my DC records, and Jeanette for her personal care and her loyalty as a DC fan; and to my Saratoga travel mate Ingrid, with whom I share a serendipitous friendship because of the Cassidy magic.

TABLE OF CONTENTS

Forward	I can hear your heartbeat: So I did this special tribute to David Cassidy	Pg 6
1	I remember April … in Saratoga Springs	Pg 12
2	Looking through the eyes of love	Pg 18
3	If ever someone needed someone: He helped 'grow' horse racing	Pg 22
4	The fans gave their love to DC, and he remembered perfectly	Pg 27
5	No Last Kiss: A lasting fan Romance and legacy	Pg 34
6	For your Shopping Bag: Bonus pics	Pg 36
About the author: I write the news … and now this special book		Pg 42

FORWARD
I can hear your heartbeat
So I did this special tribute to David Cassidy

Believing in magic: A shining moment in David Cassidy's horse racing career, standing in the winner's circle with Sweet Vendetta, the horse he owned with Shirl Penny, left, at Pimlico Race Course in Baltimore, Md., on May 16, 2008. (Rob Carr/Associated Press).

Pretty much every year for years now, Nov. 21 has been my personal day of introspection – admittedly with a focus on my ever-evolving efforts to stem the physical ravages of time. But in 2017, on the day before the U.S. lost John F. Kennedy in 1963, my vacuous birthday thoughts turned to the health of another American legend – in the entertainment arena. Suddenly, I was in crisis worry mode. David Cassidy was at the Broward Health Medical Centre in Fort Lauderdale, Fla., in critical shape, and had been for three days. And it was a personal case of six degrees of separation: around the time this music legend was entering the hospital, I was just leaving one in my home city of Toronto, Ontario – nothing serious. I would have given anything for that to have been David's case.

As I rested at home, I frantically tuned in to all forms of media – social, news, TV – to hopefully learn he was OK. I even thought of calling the hospital – being a journalist, I could get through, right?

Then, of all days, on my birthday, I learned things weren't OK.

I felt as if someone had punched me in the gut. Collectively, it seemed the world had just gone nine rounds – emotionally and physically battered. Being in the media, I know not everything you read is true, especially on Twitter, or Facebook or elsewhere in the online world of questionable "facts" and "fake news." But when it came to humble and kind "DC," as his friends-fans lovingly call him, that gut-kicking news was true. Just nine months after bravely announcing his dementia diagnosis and battle to the world, we lost him. We lost David Cassidy: The music, TV and theatre icon, charitable giver, animal lover and father of 2. He was just 67.

My mind raced. Why couldn't they get that donor liver he needed (in the end, according to reports, he died of liver and kidney failure)? How did it get to this point? His last public performance, at B.B. King Blues Club in New York City on March 4, 2017, was supposed to be his final onstage curtain call, after which he planned to finally take care of himself and get that true love that seemed to elude him (imagine!) – even though he did cherish acting and singing, most of all, because he wanted to make people get happy. If it pleased his gazillion fans to hear his and the Partridge Family's No. 1 1970 signature song *I Think I Love You* again, it pleased him. So he sang it – over and over – as well as his other signature solo and PF tunes.

But he was calling it quits (live performing, anyway) on that farewell tour, after a nearly 5-decade singing and acting career that gave his beauty and talent to the world, often, especially earlier in his entertainment dance, at the cost of having no real personal life of his own.

David, solo and with The Partridge Family, wowed music crowds over 5 decades. What hasn't been written is a book on his love of horses, until David Cassidy: Crazy Over You in Saratoga.

So when word of DC's hospitalization emerged, prayers echoed around the world. With the transition to extraterrestrial heights of my other beloved entertainer, British legend David Bowie, less than two years earlier, you could argue the other David's ascent to the heavens was on a similar or greater plane – for sure in the eyes of DC's fans.

Months after Nov. 21, 2017, the heartache and pain of seeing a first love go like that remained unbearable. Because commonly, those screaming, fainting childhood fans became lifelong ones. After filling stadiums like Wembley and arenas including New York City's Madison Square Garden (his shining moment to perform before his beloved mother Evelyn Ward and grandfather Fred) in the early 1970s and London's Royal Albert Hall in the mid-1980s, David remained robust in making music, and in theatre including on good old Broadway. For years later, he toured on his own and with others (like Monkee Micky Dolenz and Herman's Hermits' Peter Noone). But the here-today, gone-tomorrow world of music and the industry spin-doctors gave their own diagnosis of where David stood in the industry: The reluctant idol had become the forgotten idol. Oh really?

Anyone who really had a handle on his giant talent, like musician and disc jockey Timm McCoy, weren't buying it. Timm idolizes David Cassidy, and has for decades. He's the reason, in fact, Timm got into the biz in the first place. So as DC's 68th birthday approached, the big-hearted DJ, working from his Minneapolis studio, decided to dub April 12, 2018, as #DavidCassidyDay2018 – complete with 12.5 hours of music from his solo and Partridge Family days, and Timm's memories of David. The results were nothing less than astounding. Just a couple of days after the radio tribute aired (and was archived for forever listening), Timm recorded that over 22 million people had tuned in from around the world.

"No matter what decade you listen to David Cassidy in, he kicked ass in every decade," Timm says during one segment of the tribute show. "He really truly did. Everyone thought he was a passing fancy – that's what they thought about Elvis and John Lennon. David Cassidy's right up there. He was friends with all of them. He was the biggest thing in the world at one time. And then the media kind of lost grasp on him. But he kept on doing. Every decade he put out music, he would perform, he would give the audience what they wanted because he knew exactly what they wanted to hear, and that was him.

"To us, you're never a stranger in our hearts," Timm says on his tribute show, leading into David's 1990 tune *Stranger in Your Heart* from his self-titled album.

Which is precisely why I created this tribute book – for DC, and to a large extent, for his loyal and big-hearted fans. Because despite the worldwide grief, his wealth of accomplishments and constant calls (especially from his fan base) for the entertainment industry to recognize his achievements and pay homage to him, there were no immediate efforts by anyone of influence or status in his life to put together a special concert, or special publication, or special anything on any big scale. But thanks to the fans, music folks like Timm McCoy, and some regular and social media, there's more DC buzz. In Britain, where David was immensely popular, a Facebook campaign started in May 2018 to fund a memorial plaque on the Phoenix Theatre in London. As reported on www.davidcassidy.com, A&E was set to air a special two-part documentary, *David Cassidy: THE LAST SESSION,* on June 11, 2018, focusing on *Songs My Father Taught Me,* a project that was never completed because of his health. The project was being recorded out of Chicago-based Mix Kitchen.

A little David Cassidy inspiration in my room at the Brentwood Hotel in Saratoga Springs, N.Y., during my April 26-29, 2018, stay to research this memorial book as his fans prepared to honour him with a special bench ceremony May 20, 2018.

In an interview with Reel Chicago, Mix Kitchen producer Craig J. Snider noted that there were plans to do three 5-song sets, but only a handful of tunes like George Gershwin's *Summertime* and Cole Porter*'s Night and Day* were completed. "David Cassidy was an original," Craig told Reel Chicago. "He was one of the few who could manage the trifecta: stage, screen and music."

And that horse racing analogy brings me to ***David Cassidy: Crazy Over You in Saratoga – Ain't no rock 'n' roll story, it's a special tribute to the music legend's love of horses and the fans he loved.***

It's the first book written on David Cassidy since the world lost him, and I took it on at my own cost, as my way of shining a rightful light on him. My project took me to his favourite place in the world, Saratoga Springs, N.Y., from April 26-29, 2018, to explore, gather research, do interviews and take photos focusing on a specific but endearing and important part of David's life – his love of horses (breeding, racing and saving them). My idea was inspired by special and moving efforts, led by Susan Samantha Cox, a huge DC fan from Mishawaka, Indiana, to have him forever remembered in Saratoga Springs – a resort haven for more than two centuries that is also considered a U.S. horse breeding and thoroughbred racing hub. It's where David spent many summers for many years, when he wasn't in Fort Lauderdale the last dozen or so years before his transition. It was also where he went to escape the glare of the entertainment spotlight (yes, he had a bigger fan base than Elvis Presley and the Beatles in the early 1970s), and indulge in his horse breeding and racing passion.

Thanks to Susan Cox's efforts and the generous monetary donations of people around the world, including myself, a bench in his honour now permanently graces the newly renovated Cornelius Vanderbilt Whitney Courtyard (named after the late husband of race horse owner and philanthropist Marylou Whitney) at the National Museum of Racing and Hall of Fame (NMRHOF) in Saratoga Springs. Affixed to the bench is the nameplate: "In Memory of David Cassidy from his Friends and Fans." A second NMRHOF bench – also in DC's honour – was funded by his longtime friends: horse trainer Gary Contessa and Dr. Jerry Bilinski (a veterinarian who boarded the superstar's horses for many years and hosted him at his farm in North Chatham, N.Y.) and their wives. It reads: "In Memory of David Cassidy, Dr. Jerry and Darlene Bilinski, Gary and Jennifer Contessa."

Out of love, honour and gratitude for the joy David has given myself and the world, I produced *David Cassidy: Crazy Over You in Saratoga* (fans will know that *Crazy Over You* is the title of DC's heavy rock-blazing song, which lives in a demo track David played on an L.A. radio show, and was never officially released – another battle being fought by others who also strive to further David's legacy). My hope is that this booklet will touch you in ways you haven't been touched before. After all, we all know how much David loved his fans, and how they loved him back. As he said on March 3, 2017, during one of his last concerts, at the Greenwich Odeum in Rhode Island: "Thank you. For all of it. For all the decades. I don't think I do ... I *know* I love you."

(SOME NOTES: *Except where noted in photo credits, yours truly snapped all of them. The first image, a 2008 Associated Press shot of David with Sweet Vendetta in the winner's circle, is my purchase through licence from the AP's New York City office; thanks to Susan Samantha Cox and Monika Vetter-Murrel for their pics.)*

1. I remember April ... in Saratoga Springs

Daydreamer times: Candles glow in front of David Cassidy's Greatest Hits LP cover as the vinyl spins on the record player in the corner of the Brentwood Hotel bar, with a 1980s pic of the legendary singer and avid horseman also sitting on the marble countertop.

The rustic, black-panelled bar of the Brentwood Hotel this chilly April evening is filled with the sweet sound of a male songbird. From the blazing firepit just outside the front entrance to the cosy, intimate interior of the bar, the warm setting is made even steamier by the smooth, sultry voice coming from the record player tucked in the corner inside. It's an unmistakable and oh-so-present voice, with that infectious "uuuu" inflection: "You don't know how many times I wished that I had told youuuu, you don't know how many times I wished that I could hold youuuu."

Months after that heart-wrenching news of Nov. 21, 2017, David Cassidy is still making us swoon, some five decades after debuting on TV and in music to the tune of *The Partridge Family,* and as a solo concert phenomenon on countless stages around the world. This damp April evening, my friend and I skipped *Walking in the Rain* to spin some DC vinyl, and soak in some of his most endearing and enduring tunes.

But the purpose of visiting picturesque Saratoga Springs wasn't to capture his musical magic, although listening to that golden voice is always a spiritual awakening. Checking into the Brentwood Hotel, just across the street from the historic Saratoga Race Course, I wanted to explore another important side of David Cassidy, who lived in Saratoga for several warm-weather weeks over many years to nurture the other part of his soul – his love of horses. It's where he would get away from the often frenzied, cutthroat business of show business – although he also saw horse racing as another form of entertainment.

"There are no guarantees about anything and that at any moment, anything can happen. You can be sitting on top of the world one day and the next day you are sweeping it. But that's part of the thrill, and I'm a thrill-seeker," he said in a 2002 article in The Daily Racing Form, now a New York City-based multi-platform media and e-commerce company that reports on horse racing.

In 1994's *C'mon, Get Happy ... Fear and Loathing on the Partridge Family Bus,* he admits enduring some frustration, "heartaches and disappointment" while he "indulged in my passion for breeding thoroughbred racehorses. Though I still love horses, I'm essentially out of the racehorse game for now because I know I cannot stand the pain and frustration any longer. It seemed like I had a number of chances to really hit the jackpot with horse racing but somehow I never did. It always eluded me. The best horses I owned would break their legs or something else with a one-in-a-thousand chance of happening would happen." But he returned to the horse racing and breeding fold, because to David, it wasn't just about the thrill of victory and the agony of defeat – it was also another aspect of his love of animals and nature. Even as he was being chased by frenetic girls as a "teen idol" – a term he abhorred and that couldn't even begin to scrape the scope of his talents and impact on his fans and music – there were times he longed for those *Summer Days* of skinny dipping, roughing it and anonymous living. Saratoga became his sanctuary – instead of being chased by fans, it was the four-legged beauties doing the chasing to the finish line. Horses soothed David from the time he was kindergarten age, around the time his parents, actors Jack Cassidy and Evelyn Ward, split (something not told to David right away).

I nicknamed the pony on the left Bowie (with the 2 different-coloured eyes and Ziggy-inspired red hair) and the chestnut beauty on the right DC, which seems to be rocking David's mid-1980s look. (Ingrid B.)

"I've always had a love for horses since I was really young," said DC, who was born David Bruce Cassidy in New York City and grew up in West Orange, N.J. "When I was 5 years old, the only thing that made me happy was when they'd take me out and give me pony rides." It's a sentiment that was top of my mind as my friend Ingrid and I came across 3 ponies grazing in the backyard of a home just down the street from the Brentwood Hotel while we were out for a walk one afternoon. Two of the ponies sauntered right up to us at the chain-link fence. They reminded me of my top 2 music icons, both named David: Bowie (because of its tousled red hair and two different-coloured eyes) and DC (with the chocolate brown coat and blond-tinged hair that reminded me of his 1980s *Romance* album days). Even more heart stopping was the name of the street kitty corner to the backyard where the ponies were grazing: Ward Street (I could only think of David's mother Evelyn).

David's granddad, Evelyn's father, was especially influential in shaping his horse passion. David recalled in interviews about how he went to live with his grandfather and grandmother, Ethel Laurinda Ward, in New Jersey, and how he accompanied his sports-loving granddad to the race track when he was just 10.

Five years later, he bought his first riding horse, after he and his mother moved to California. It was in Saratoga Springs, in 1974 near the tail end of his Partridge Family career and while he was still tearing up concert venues, that he purchased his first yearling – at the Fasig-Tipton sales pavilion, the start of an annual love affair with Saratoga that lasted some four decades, and put him in the winner's circle several times.

'I've had a passion for horses since I was very young – I used to sit on the floor in front of the races on television and pretend to be a jockey – and I first began reading the racing form on the set of The Partridge Family.' – David Cassidy

---

David's life as an entertainer was a whirlwind. He wanted to be an actor, following in his parents' footsteps. His first job was on the theatre stage in *The Fig Leaves Are Falling*, for just a few days in January 1969; he went on to do numerous TV shows before landing *The Partridge Family* role of Keith, the eldest of five, featuring his stepmom Shirley Jones. The producers of the series, which lasted four years, hit the jackpot: David could act, AND sing AND play instruments, and went on to drive the group. Through the decades, his fan base stuck by his side. Even after Nov. 21, 2017, the sexy warmth and the burning desire to envelop yourself in David's music and smile never disappeared for his fans. And it seems like there are gazillions of them to this day (witness the dizzying array of fan pages), most of them from the time they were those fainting, screaming young concert-goers.

Now, I could have written a tribute book on a range of David's other unique traits and accomplishments, like his heartthrob looks (smouldering hazel eyes and that hair – from a long, feathery dark brown shag that evolved into '80s bleach-blonde and, later, a carefully groomed shorter cut); the indelible mark he made on music (album-wise, more

The bronze Native Dancer statue, by Centennial Park at Union Avenue and Circular Street, was vandalized in recent years. Two men, who rode the statue like a rocking horse, pleaded guilty early in 2016 to misdemeanor charges.

than a dozen with The Partridge Family, and nearly three dozen solo, with platinum and gold sales), television, the theatre stage (from his launch in 1969's *The Fig Leaves are Falling*, to *Blood Brothers* in the mid-1990s and beyond) and in Las Vegas (headlining the elaborate and magical EFX from 1997-99); his record-breaking concerts (from the early seventies to his emotional farewell tour that ended in New York City); and the massive number of times he graced teen and other magazines.

But that ground has been covered before – wall to wall – including by David's still-flourishing official website (www.davidcassidy.com, which is maintained by a web team, with contributions from loyal fans); on social media, including through @CassidyUnited; past newspaper and magazine articles, and the numerous TV and public appearances he made during his career; and even David's own memoirs (1994's *C'mon, Get Happy ... Fear and Loathing on the Partridge Family Bus* and 2007's *Could It Be Forever? My Story*). What hasn't been covered in any depth is the extraordinary efforts of some of David's friends and fans to honour him when others didn't.

As DC would say, "Happy trails," as you relive Cassidymania, this time in Saratoga, through my words and pictures, and the words of those who knew and loved David, in the coming pages.

2. Looking through the eyes of love
She turned around and it was, 'Oh my God, David!'

Matt McCabe's Saratoga Guitar & Music Center on Broadway features cool guitars, collector vinyl records and other items for music lovers. He opened his business in June 1994, has two Saratoga Springs locations and has met numerous celebrities, including David Cassidy.

When I started out on my first journey to Saratoga Springs, I had two goals: To soak in the same atmosphere David lived and breathed during his several weeks there each year, and to ask anyone I could about the impact David had on this community and horse racing.

First, a lowdown on Saratoga's rich history, which can be traced back to the 14th century, and why it's come to be known as the Queen of the Spas, and a gambling and resort destination.

The area was known as Serachtague ("place of swift water") and was sacred to the

Mohawks and other native Americans who believed the naturally carbonated water had been stirred by the god Manitou, giving it healing properties. It grew and evolved into the city of Saratoga Springs, and by the mid-1800s, became the home of many wealthy Americans and people from other countries. It also evolved into a key U.S. racing hub. The Saratoga Race Course, built by John Hunter, the first chairman of The Jockey Club, and William R. Travers, opened on Aug. 3, 1863. Originally across from Union Avenue, it is now on massive grounds at 267 Union, and is one of the oldest race courses in the United States. Over the decades, spectators at the Saratoga track have taken in the likes of horses as famous as Secretariat (David's all-time favourite), Seattle Slew, Affirmed and Man o' War (all holding a place in the National Museum of Racing and Hall of Fame). Just down the street, at 191 Union, is the NMRHOF. I predict the museum-hall of fame will become an even bigger drawing card because of the two David Cassidy memorial benches, which helped complete the newly renovated Cornelius Vanderbilt Whitney Courtyard (named after the late husband of Saratoga icon Marylou Whitney) in May 2018.

Today, Saratoga Springs has a population of about 27,000 that swells during the summer thoroughbred racing season, which starts in July and attracts hearty crowds through Labour Day. It's also an in-demand setting for weddings and a restaurant-goer's haven. During my time in this idyllic city, where I settled into a charming room at the Brentwood Hotel, right across the street from the race course, it was clear that despite not being physically here, David has remained "a hero, a giant, a man who's as tall as can be" in Saratoga County, the charming upstate New York region framed by the Adirondack mountains and featuring beautiful lakes and rivers.

"I've never picked him up for a ride, but of course I know of him – people talk about him here all the time," says my Uber driver, who on this day was taking me to Saratoga Springs's historic downtown area along Broadway street. One of the first places I dropped into was a guitar store: someone in there would know DC, I thought. Sure enough, Matt McCabe, the owner of Saratoga Guitar & Music Center, who opened his business in June 1994, recounted the first time the guitar whiz came into his store, around 1996. Matt's sister, longtime DC fan Meredith, happened to be with the music shop owner.

"The first time I met him," recalls Matt of DC, "he came over to the City Centre the weekend of our first guitar show … and he just came walking in. I recognized him right away and my sister happened to be visiting. … it was kind of neat because growing up it was kind of one of those crush things. So I said, 'Meredith, you remember David Cassidy?' She turned around and it was, 'Oh, my God, David. Oh David.' He obviously gets that all the time, but he was nice about it.

"He was just very pleasant and I told him about the guitar show. He said, 'I like Gretches [a type of guitar],' and throughout the years when he was in town, he probably stopped in

David Cassidy would pop into the Saratoga Guitar & Music Center on Broadway once in a while, showing music wasn't far from his mind even in horse-crazy Saratoga.

here about a half-dozen times. … I met a lot of very famous people, and it's always nice to meet somebody like that. … it was kind of cool my sister was able to meet him."

When David would come into the store, he "would pick up different guitars and he would play, just strum them all," Matt tells me. "He wasn't trying to be flashy or anything. He was just passing the time."

But there was one special visit: when David was looking to buy a guitar for his son.

"He was on the phone with him for an hour trying to get something for his son, saying, 'Look, I want to get you this, I know the holidays are coming up.' And I would hear this conversation go on for well over an hour." He believes David ended up getting that special instrument for Beau, who was living outside New York at the time.

The last time Matt saw David was about three years ago, when he stopped into the shop owner's other location. "He popped in and just grabbed a guitar and was looking around. He did like talking about guitars – and then he had the horses."

The Log Jam Restaurant in Lake George, about a 45-minute drive from Saratoga, one of David's favourite eateries, is famous for its steak and seafood.

The day before my guitar-store visit, I had my first visit to the National Museum of Racing and Hall of Fame, when I was graciously allowed to view David's memorial bench from the fans and the Contessa-Bilinski one. At the front desk, Sue (that name seems to permeate David's life!) spilled story after story about him. Sue says he gave his time generously to help raise money for CAPTAIN Youth and Family Services, including at a summer gala where she met him. More telling of his popularity is the calls that she fielded

David lived in Saratoga during the summer racing season. This is one of his former homes.

at the NMRHOF during her work hours, from emotional fans. "Don't you understand, it's David Cassidy,'" one woman, practically in tears, said to Sue. David's ability to make fans cry, and even laugh, is still there. Take John, the waiter who served my friend and I at the Log Jam Restaurant in Lake George, an Adirondack region town north of Saratoga Springs. We decided to dine one night at the log cabin-style steak and seafood restaurant because David ate there frequently. In fact, we learned from John that David's son was friends with the son of Logjam general manager Tony Grecco. As for the laughing part, once John discovered I was doing this tribute book, he pulled out the guitar-shaped dessert menu, and started singing, "Come on get fatty."

3. If ever someone needed someone
David helped 'grow' the sport of horse racing

The National Museum of Racing and Hall of Fame in Saratoga Springs was founded in 1950 to honour thoroughbreds, jockeys, trainers and others in the sport. The 2 benches in memory of David Cassidy now grace the newly renovated courtyard. (Courtesy of NMRHOF)

It's the weekend before the biggest race, so far, of the year, the Kentucky Derby (won May 5 by favourite Justify), and the sport's aficionados in Saratoga take the first race in the Triple Crown just as seriously as those right at Churchill Downs in Louisville. The race is commonly referred to as "The Greatest Two Minutes in Sports."

On Saturday, April 28, the "Countdown to the Triple Crown: Kentucky Derby Preview Panel," featuring racing experts Tom Amello and Michael Veitch, was held in the NMRHOF's massive Hall of Fame room. Lining the hall's walls are thousands of plaques commemorating noted personalities in horse racing history, from the jockeys and trainers to the horses (names like Seattle Slew and DC fave Secretariat, which, in 1973, at the height of Cassidymania, became the first Triple Crown winner in 25 years). There's also a Hall of Fame "Pillars of the Turf" category for individuals who have made extraordinary contributions to horse racing, and a fan movement is afoot to get David Cassidy that recognition. During the question-and-answer session of the panel discussion, Tom responded to an audience member's comment on the role of celebrities in promoting thoroughbred racing. Before the about 120 in attendance, he said to her that while celebrities aren't the main drivers of the sport, they can add profile to it, and "David Cassidy helped grow the game."

The Saratoga Race Course season begins in July and lasts until Labour Day, a period when the number of people in Saratoga Springs swells past the regular 27,000 population.

Now, Tom was looking directly at me when he made that comment about David, because part of the reason I was there was to hear more about the contributions he made to the sport. Tom is a retired teacher, longtime Saratoga handicapper and horse-racing expert, and also owner with his daughter Kate Amello of the Brunswick at Saratoga Bed & Breakfast, just down the street from the museum-Hall of Fame on Union Avenue. Tom gave this account of how the entertainment superstar left it all on the track when it came to promoting the sport he loved.

"I'd see him in the boxes during the races. I'd also see him in the backstretch. There were a couple of television programs there and David was very generous of his time, and he would often appear on TV. This is an interesting game nowadays because most people came to the game through a father, or an uncle or someone who took them to the track. In the world of simulcasting, people don't go to the track as often as they used to. There are a lot of other options for gambling … and so David Cassidy was the kind of personality with a following from his TV shows and his touring who when interviewed here, and when given the opportunity to promote his passion and interest of the game,

The Hall of Fame part of the NMRHOF houses plaques and exhibits that pay tribute to the greats in thoroughbred racing. David Cassidy was the keynote speaker at the 2005 hall induction ceremony, saying, 'I want to be an ambassador for this sport.'

gave freely of his time and really helped promote what is the New York state breeding program.

"People like David Cassidy who love the game are instrumental in promoting the game," adds Tom, "the folks in the New York breeding program, the trainers, the owners' association, he was a contributor and he deserved the recognition they were giving him." In fact, David has made his share of appearances at the Hall of Fame, where Tom was on the derby panel this day. In 2005, the singing superstar was the keynote speaker at the induction ceremony for trainer Nick Zito. During his speech, David, who also happened to have a horse in a race that day, wowed the crowd with stories about his entertainment career while also speaking about his love of racing: "The passion that I have has been with me since I was a little boy. ... I love this game. I want to be an ambassador for this sport. We need an ambassador, we need a face. I would love to be able to help in any way I can."

David was also active in fundraising for horse charities, including the Thoroughbred Retirement Foundation, which helps save retired horses from harm and slaughter. According to www.davidcassidy.com, his other charitable efforts included signing items for auction and performing concerts at picnic fundraisers in 2010 and 2011 in North Chatham, N.Y., to support animal welfare causes. One of his most notable fundraisers was the 2006 Julien's auction in Los Angeles that raised tens of thousands of dollars (some of it going to the horse protection cause) and featured items like his Partridge Family memorabilia and some 1970s, flashy Manuel stage costumes. Tom wasn't surprised about David's efforts to sustain horses in retirement: "People who own horses, respect horses, and do everything they can to sustain the horse that served them so well."

Also helping oversee the derby panel this day was Brien Bouyea, the museum-Hall of Fame's communications director, who, along with director of development Cate Johnson, experienced much of the fan excitement over the memorial bench that the fans were helping make a reality. "We had people approach us and say obviously David Cassidy has such a love for horse racing and such a love for Saratoga, and you have so many passionate fans, they thought the museum would be a great place to pay a little tribute to him, his legacy, and his love for Saratoga and love for horse racing … the fans really just fed into this," says Brien. "You can tell what passionate fans David has the way this has all come out, and they've been with him through the decades. He's one of the few [decades-long entertainers] who I think the fans stayed with. That shows a lot."

The second bench, as mentioned earlier, was donated by David's friends, trainer Gary Contessa and veterinarian Jerry Bilinski. Brien says he would speak to Gary about his relationship with David, "and he just said you will not have a guy who just loves this sport more. It's great they also showed their support for him and it's just been a win-win for everybody, and they have a great space in that courtyard." For his part, Gary trained noted horses owned or co-owned by David, including Sweet Vendetta, which won the 2008 Black-Eyed Susan Stakes. David's other horses included five-time stakes winner Half Heaven, and stakes winners Dolly Baby, Jenny's So Great and Citrus Kid. He named another favourite Mayan King, after the street that housed his former mansion in Fort Lauderdale, Fla.

Gary has expressed in the days after Nov. 21, 2017, how much he admired David's knowledge of horses and racing. He told the thoroughbred racing publication BloodHorse that he spoke to David about a week before that day. "We had a long conversation. The horses were his escape from the crazy life he had in rock and roll. He was the consummate student of [horse] pedigrees. I don't think anybody's smarter than him when it came to pedigrees and breeding. He was an incredible student of the game."

4. The fans gave their love to DC, and he remembered perfectly

Sneak preview on April 28, 2018, of the pine bench from DC's fans. I added albums to marry his music and horse passions (the standalone bench pic is coming up!). Top left is a blowup of the nameplate. The fan bench and another donated one grace the NMRHOF's renovated Cornelius Vanderbilt Whitney Courtyard (in the background, featuring bronze Secretariat statue by John Skeaping), named after the late husband of Saratoga icon Marylou Whitney. May 17, 2018, was the official opening event, with the fan day May 20.

At the height of Cassidymania, circa early 1970s Partridge Family days, David would commonly leave his concerts with a hoarse voice from trying to sing above fans' screams. He'd bound off the stage at the end of most shows, and get whisked away by security to a waiting vehicle. Commonly, he'd wrap himself in a blanket to gain that security he longed for after each high-energy, frenetic show.

"I knew the fans loved me – they didn't want to kill me – but their emotions were at fever pitch," he writes in *C'Mon Get Happy … Fear and Loathing on the Partridge Family Bus*, which also chronicles story after story of fans camping outside his work or home, even hiding in his hotel rooms.

He always loved his fans, though, and later in his life, he came to embrace them even more. In *C'Mon Get Happy*, written when David was in his mid-40s, he confesses to enjoying singing the Partridge Family songs he once undervalued. "I even enjoy, I honestly do, singing all the old songs that in 1974 I was sure I'd never wanted to sing again. … I realized that they brought their share of happiness to people." So he'd sing them at all his concerts. His fans? A bulk of them were the same ones who once rushed the stages, screamed and fainted, and were still following him to concert venues around the world. Over the years, he'd gain new followers as he bounded from TV (*The Partridge Family, David Cassidy: Man Undercover*) and the music stage, to theatre, and TV again in *Ruby and the Rockits* and *Celebrity Apprentice*, all the while singing to make people happy. And it was the fans, staying by his side even through his difficult times, who first moved to get a permanent tribute in place following the tragic news of Nov. 21, 2017. Enter Susan Samantha Cox, the Indiana resident who led the movement for the memorial bench at the NMRHOF, a core team of volunteers from the U.S. and Canada, and an army of fans who donated to the special fundraising campaign.

There was no way Susan and other fans in David's army would let things lie when it came to some sort of concrete memorial for the man who brought so much joy into their lives, over so many years. So Susan's New Year's resolution for Jan. 1, 2018, was to find something special to honour him. "I knew Saratoga Springs, New York, was his favourite place," she says. "I knew he was a horse breeder and involved in horse racing, but also cared and believed in protecting retired thoroughbreds. I called all over Saratoga and finally through contacting the National Museum of Racing and Hall of Fame, found a place for David's memorial bench."

Within two weeks of launching the fundraising campaign, by Jan. 30, the bench was paid for, and the donations kept pouring in. DC fans have their own unique stories about why he means so much to them. Susan Cox never got to one of his concerts, but her friend managed to snag a guitar pick for her that David had dropped during a performance in 2007 at the Indiana State Fair. Then there's Susan's recollections of how David's music gave her solace while growing up.

"I owe my life to my grandparents and David Cassidy. I truly would not have survived childhood without them," says Susan (shown on the left as she is today, and during Cassidymania in the smaller photos, with her guitar on the left and her DC-style shaggy hair in the right corner). Her grandparents, she says, stepped in when her parents didn't; David stepped off the TV screen (as far back as 1969) and the stage to give her strength. She even took up the guitar because of him.

But it's her story about how she reached out to David after his dad Jack died in a fire at his home in December 1976 that solidified her connection with him. "Shortly after his father's death, David discussed his fractured relationship with his dad," she recalls. "Since I understand about parental rejection, I … wrote him a letter … I told him that I saw him speak about his relationship with his dad. I told him I felt his pain … I told him that he was an amazing person and I know he would do great things. I told him that I understood how deep his pain was. I was not expecting to hear back; some time passed. To my surprise, I got a letter from David. He thanked me and said he felt comfort in knowing both that someone cared enough to write and knew his pain. I felt strength from his words. Knowing how David impacted my life and knowing how he often spoke of loving his fans, I found comfort in his music. He gave over 47 years to his fans. It was time for us to give something back to him. He needed a permanent memorial place where fans could visit and share a moment of tribute to him."

The fundraising campaign for the bench was just one small part of banding David's fans together in their ever-vigilant efforts to keep him in everyone's thoughts, and earn him the accolades that his fans believe he deserves (like Rock and Roll Hall of Fame entry, and a star on the Hollywood Walk of Fame). Susan Cox started a "David Cassidy Memorial Bench" Facebook page that quickly garnered hundreds of "likes," and keeps fans abreast of David happenings, including leading up to May 20, 2018, when fans could go to the newly spruced up courtyard for free for two hours to see the benches first-hand. For Susan, one of the most heartening parts about the bench campaign was bringing David's fans "together," albeit even just virtually, to share stories of how he has impacted their lives and keep his legacy burning. The bench unveiling May 20 was to be the first time Susan would meet dozens of David lovers she had been chatting with online for months.

This fan-sponsored bench in the NMRHOF along with another bench dedicated to David are in the Cornelius Vanderbilt Whitney Courtyard, and are sure to attract fans of the entertainment superstar. How fitting that the two benches share the courtyard with the bronze statue of 1973 Triple Crown winner Secretariat, David's favourite horse. The statue was created by sculptor John Skeaping in 1974 and gifted by Paul Mellon. A special campaign also allowed people to buy bricks and have them engraved and placed in the courtyard.

A few of those fans formed a core team (Linda de Ambrosio from Orange County, Calif., Monika Vetter-Murrel from Carstairs, Alberta, and Erica Brenner of Cincinnati, Ohio) to help organize activities to coincide with the courtyard unveiling, including a Celebration of Life Event for David, at The Parting Glass, an Irish pub David frequently popped into. Given his Irish roots (his dad was half-Irish and half-German, his mom Irish and Swiss), The Parting Glass was the perfect backdrop for the Celebration of Life.

At the courtyard gathering, the organizers were set to read their unique, heartfelt, emotional stories on how David touched their lives. Here are parts of them (taken from the notes each sent to Susan and passed on to me for this special booklet), which at times made me tear up:

Linda de Ambrosio: "Living with three generations in one household, like David, I was fortunate to have had my grandparents in my life. My parents were also loving parents, but busy at work to make a living. My dad was away at sea mostly, as a merchant marine. When he would arrive back from a trip, we would pick him up at the dock. Who would know that this experience served me well when I learned the Partridges were filming a segment aboard a cruise ship that would soon be docking at a local port. Of course, I made my way down to the dock. If ever there was a time when it was necessary to have the faith of a grain of a mustard seed, it was now. It has been said that good things come to those who wait – and that it did. Just like the opening of each segment of *The Partridge Family*, where the Partridges made their way across the screen, life imitated art. There they were, one by one, each Partridge coming off the ship. There David was so gracious and generous with his time, especially after what was a very exhausting trip … I asked him to autograph a piece of thin airmail paper that was previously signed by David and on more than one occasion. When he said, 'This will be the last time,' I was devastated to hear those words because it sounded so final. It must have been written all over my face as he quickly said, 'on that piece of paper.' I so treasure that moment and his sensitivity to my feelings that he felt he needed to quickly clarify. Ask and you shall receive. That's what I did. I was so happy to have the opportunity to have *The Partridge Family* come into my living room every week, but I wanted so much to go into theirs. I asked David if I could visit *The Partridge Family* set and there I was within weeks on Veterans Day 1973 for taping during the last season."

Erica Brenner: My folks knew how much I loved David Cassidy and for my 10th birthday (July 7, 1972), took my sister and me to see him Aug. 27, 1972, at Blossom Music Center in Cleveland, Ohio. We had a picnic prior to the show and the memory of being together as a family was incredibly special. Right before the show started, my dad decided not to sit in the pavilion area. He said he wanted to watch from the lawn. We were in fantastic seats. But, soon discovered, it didn't matter where we were. SOMETHING was about to happen!! The announcer came on stage, gave us the routine information about restroom locations, parking and fire evacuation procedures. David Cassidy's introduction was followed by a wild stampede of 'humans.' The people behind us jumped over rows of seats, pushing and shoving to get closer to the stage. The audience shouting was deafening and all I could see was David, on stage, in a white jumpsuit, as he moved around on stage, with incredible energy. At one point, my sister Ruth, only six years old, started crying and I almost did. Instead, I told my mom I was really scared. I remember mom reassuring my sister and me that no one would jump over or on top of us if we are sitting. Then she asked if I wanted to leave. I said yes and asked when. I remember her saying we would go when it was safe enough to escape. She gave the go-ahead and we made a beeline for my father who was standing just outside the pavilion, where he said he'd be. My sister was worn out and fell asleep as soon as my dad started driving the car. My mom turned to me in the back seat and asked if I had a good time. I told her I loved being together as a family and enjoyed the picnic. I thanked my parents for the chance to see David. I also asked if all rock concerts were like that one. My mom asked what I meant. I said … where the artist is on stage, you can't hear the performer and ordinary people turn crazy. … The David Cassidy show was NOT like anything we experienced."

Monika Vetter-Murrel: "Back in 1972 there was a contest to win tickets from the radio station. I tried so hard to win, because I knew I could never afford to go see him. … I was the fifth caller and was ecstatic to have won the tickets! However, I was in the nosebleed section, but it didn't matter, there he was!!! I soon learned to play guitar and bought every music book that I was able to afford once I started working. I always dreamed of singing with David someday and many a fantasy led me on that stage with him. Over the years I listened to his music when I could, and once the internet became available I looked him up and found his website. I was thrilled … finally I could see there were many more CD's available. I bought all that I could. Years later, I was visiting my family in Toronto and found out that David was putting on an outdoor concert in Peterborough, Ontario. I was so excited. My friend who was supposed to go with me couldn't, but that didn't stop me. I went anyway! It was pouring rain all day… I took an umbrella, and made sure I had a good coat and off I went! I can't tell you the excitement I felt when I knew soon I would see him and this time I was close enough to see him completely! I felt tears well up in me as he walked out on stage. All my childhood memories flooded back. The love I felt for him in those days, all flooded back … it was marvellous. I got up to the front of the stage and was just thrilled to see him that close! Years went by again, and then I heard he was coming to Calgary, to a casino that my pastor's wife's brother managed … I prayed with all my heart that I would get to meet him. I was the very first one to buy tickets… got front-row centre. Talk about close. I could rest my feet on the speakers that were in front of the stage. The best part however was that I was given the go-ahead to go backstage!!!! I found my 57-year-old self calming the 14-year-old in me a lot! I was however amazingly calm when he walked out to meet me. I didn't faint or cry (I was sure I would). I was able to tell him how he had inspired music in me, and that I was a recording artist and worship leader now, and I had a CD of my songs for him.... He was genuinely grateful, telling me how wonderful it is that I did that for him, got to get my picture taken with him and asked if I could give him a hug ... he said of course, and I tell ya, that was the best hug I ever got! Now instead of David's smile on my bedroom wall, I have both of our smiles together in a frame, a day I will never forget."

5. No Last Kiss: A lasting fan Romance & legacy

Evelyn Ward
(May 21, 1923 - Dec 23, 2012)

David's fans mourn the passing of his mother, Evelyn Ward.

We give thanks to David for continuing to be the voice for victims of Alzheimer's and dementia and their families.

As long as there's you: The fans even stepped up for David Cassidy's mother, actress Evelyn Ward. He took care of her for many years before her passing in 2012 after battling Alzheimer's.

On my last night in Saratoga, I slipped into my hotel room, where a DC album, shirt and book lined my table, and noticed a note on Brentwood Hotel paper on my freshly made bed (see Page 37). It read: "Just want to say I'm a big fan of David Cassidy. He's my all time favorite actor/singer." It was signed by Jeanette in housekeeping. Turns out, her boyfriend used to train David's horses.

Jeanette's passion is exactly the reaction I found everywhere I went in Saratoga. If someone didn't meet David Cassidy in person, there was a story of kindness, giving and humour somewhere there.

His legacy lives on not just in his horse-related efforts, music, and rich TV, film and theatre work, but also in his charitable work. His generosity is contagious. Over the months after his transition, numerous online and other charitable efforts to honour David sprung up, in part to aid the causes he embraced most, like helping retired thoroughbred horses and unravelling the mysteries of dementia. For my part, I will be donating a chunk of the proceeds from the sale of ***David Cassidy: Crazy Over You in Saratoga*** to a charity supporting research, preferably preventive research, into dementia and Alzheimer's. Here's a little bit of info on the challenges faced by people living with dementia: it affects the brain, behaviour and mood, and can cause declining mental ability to the point it interferes with daily living. Alzheimer's accounts for the bulk of dementia cases. With our aging population, the number of people around the world living with dementia is estimated at 47 million and is projected to rise to 75 million by 2030, according to the World Health Organization.

David gave freely of his time to raise money for the Alzheimer's Association, and was a vigorous spokesperson after his grandfather Fred struggled with it, and while he was caring for his mother, who died of dementia at age 89 on Dec. 23, 2012. He was diagnosed with it just five years later, at age 66. When he announced he would stop performing onstage, he said: "I want to focus on what I am and how I've been without any distractions. I want to love. I want to enjoy life."

To his fans, living and loving isn't quite the same these days, but that isn't stopping them from continuing to find ways to honour him, and believing that yes, David, heaven's road is paved with gold. As Susan Cox said to me: "I know David is smiling in heaven and sees the love we fans have and how we will remain his fans. David, you truly saved my life. I love you and I always will. Could it be forever? Yes David, it is."

'It's really important that we talk about Alzheimer's and dementia now because in the next few years, it's gonna be such an issue. ... There are a lot of people that are alone that would like to contribute to our society." – David Cassidy

---

6. For your Shopping Bag: Bonus pics

The letters received by each person who donated to David's memorial bench at the NRMHOF.

The Brentwood Hotel welcoming sign, and the letter from housekeeper Jeanette that touched my heart.

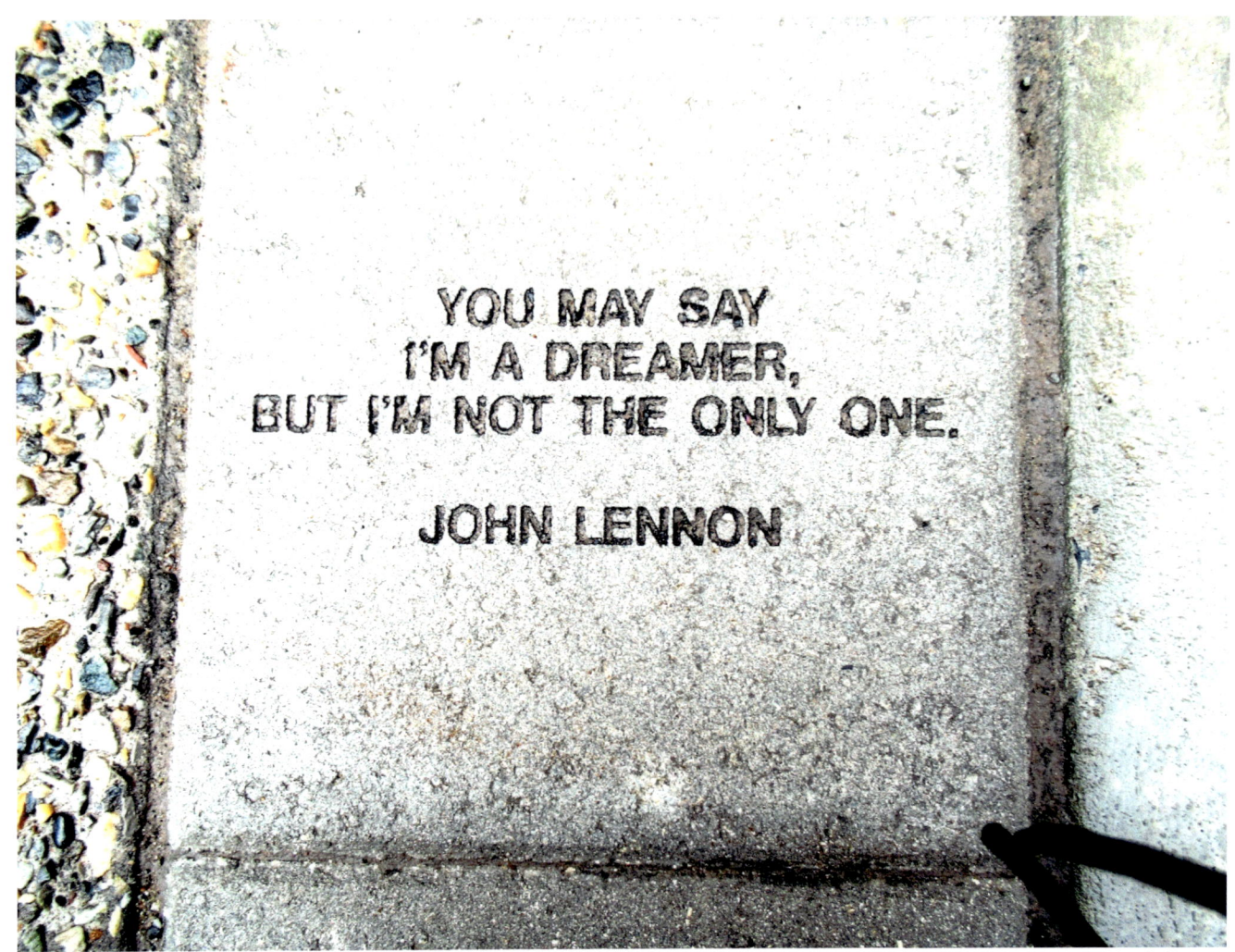

The sidewalk and entranceway outside Caffe Lena, which opened in 1960 and is a noted folk music venue in a 19th-century building in historic downtown Saratoga Springs. The late Beatle and legendary John Lennon, a friend of David Cassidy, is one of the many artists and individuals honoured on the walkway and sidewalk outside the café. I think of David's Daydreamer song when I read this message from his friend.

My first horse sighting, a nagging photobomb, actually, after landing at the Albany airport en route to DC country: Saratoga Springs.

Ingrid and I warming up to the bench that fans dedicated to David. It was a surreal and heart-pounding experience seeing it and sitting on it for the first time.

Hazel eyes 'you're beautiful, this song's for you. If words could paint a picture, there'd be no words to say.'

About the author
I write the news … and now this special book

My journalism career has been a blessing that has allowed me to research, cover, meet and write about people and happenings that touch individuals, communities and the world. Born in Swift Current, Sask., and raised in a Lebanese immigrant family of 14 children (my parents were busy), my dream to become a sports writer took me to the Globe and Mail in Toronto after graduating from Ryerson University. Two years later, I joined The Canadian Press as a reporter. Since October 2005, I have been working at the Canadian Broadcasting Corporation (CBC) as an online reporter and editor. Health is wealth, so as an aside to my journalism career, I run a fitness business, and help people change their lives in another way. **David Cassidy: Crazy Over You in Saratoga** is my personal passion project and first book. It's been a privilege writing about a legend.

Made in the USA
Columbia, SC
29 November 2024